My

Tool

Box

By

Bruce Dolan Smith

1st Edition

Published by BDS Distributors

Copyright 2018 by BDS Distributors

Introduction

Whenever an emergency pops up with me I always have problems getting all of the stuff I need. This tool box will be a good start on getting organized with all of your medications, important information and what to do when an emergency does pop up with you. This tool box is about you and all of the information that you want to share.

When filling out your Wellness Tool box take your time and do one step at time.

A Prayer to Start Your Day

Dear Lord,

I cannot do this alone

O God, early in the morning I cry to you

Help me to pray

And to concentrate my thoughts on you

I cannot do this alone

In me there is darkness

But with you there is light

I am lonely, but you do not leave me

I am feeble in heart, but with you there is help

I am restless, but with you there is peace

In me there is bitterness, but with you there is

patience

I do not understand your ways

But you know the way for me

Restore me to liberty

And enable me to live now

That I may answer before you and before me

Lord, whatever this day may bring

Your name be praised

Amen

Table of Contents

Chapter 1

Important information

Name____

Address_______________________________________

____

City ____

State__________Zip_______________________

Phone Number___________________________________

Email Address__________________________________

DOB____/_____/________

Medical Insurance

1 Company_______________________________________

Policy Number____________________________________

2 Company_______________________________________

Policy Number____________________________________

Chapter 2

Medical Information

Primary Doctor________________________________

Address________________________________

City________________________________

State________ Zip__________

Phone Number__________________

Doctors Information

Doctors Name_______________________________________

Address____

City____

State___________Zip____________

Phone number______________________________

Doctors Name_______________________________________

Address____

City____

State______________Zip________________

Phone Number______________________________

Make a list of the medications you are

prescribed by your doctors. Write the name of

the medication and dosage.

Prescription Name	Dosage

Prescription	Dosage

Prescription Name	Dosage

Allergies____

____

Chapter 3

What are my symptom early warning signs and

triggers?

Check off those that apply to you

Depression:

- o Sad, crying most of the day, nearly every

  day

- o Irritable,

- o Avoiding pleasure actives once enjoyed

- o Changes in appetite or body weight

- o Sleeping too much or not able to sleep

- o Feelings of restlessness

- o Fatigue, loss of energy, exhaustion

- o Not able to make decisions or concentrate

- o Thoughts of death or suicide

Mania

- o Feeling abnormally energetic, having too much energy, feeling better than good

- o Unusually irritable for more than a week

- o High self-esteem, like you can do anything

- o Decreased in sleep without feeling tired.

- o More talkative than normal.

- o Racing thoughts, too many ideas coming in at one time

- o Distracted easily, jumping for topic to topic

- o Restlessness, increase in making goals,

  wanting to do more than normal

- o Excessive pursuit of pleasure without

  thinking of the consequences

Other Symptoms:

- o Drinking or using recreational drugs

- o Overeating

- o Obsessions

- o Anxiety

- o Panic attack

- o Delusions or strange and bizarre thoughts

- o Hallucinations such as seeing or hearing

  things that are not there

- o Grandiose Ideations

o   Paranoia

Write down your own early warning signs and

triggers: _______________________________

____

____

____

____

____

____

____

____

Now make a list of events or circumstances that

could bring on a trigger to increase your

symptoms:_______________________________

____

____

____

____

____

____

____

____

On this page write down what you can do when your triggers start to bring on symptoms:

____

____

____

____

____

____

____

____

____

Chapter 4

Getting prepared for a Crisis

It is a good idea that you are prepared should you have a crisis. This way you will know what to do.

What if I become suicidal? Remember suicidal thoughts are only temporary. If you feel suicidal call someone to talk to. This will help you get your mind busy and off the negative thinking. I always say suicide is a permanent solution to a temporary problem. All problems are only temporary. If you lose a girl friend or boyfriend think to yourself there are more out there in the world for me. I will find the right

person when the timing is right. Try not to be

alone when you are feeling this way. If need be

go to the hospital but by all means this is not the

time to be alone. Call your doctor right away

and let them know how you are feeling. Make a

promise to yourself that you will get help when

you first start to feel suicidal. Write down on

the next page a list of people you can notify

should you feel this way. Is there a support

group that you can either call or attend a meeting

during this time?

Chapter 5

Contact information

Name_______________________________________

Address____________________________________

City__________________State___Zip_________

Phone number_______________________________

Relationship________________________________

Name_______________________________________

Address_____________________________________

City__________________State___Zip_________

Phone number_______________________________

Relationship________________________________

Name_______________________________________

Address_____________________________________

City__________________State___Zip_________

Phone number_______________________________

Relationship________________________________

Name____

Address_______________________________________

City_________________________State___Zip_________

Phone number__________________________________

Relationship___________________________________

Chapter 6

Mood Triggers

People have different triggers in life that can

bring on symptoms such as panic attacks,

anxiety, depression. The below exercise will

help you thru the negative triggers in your life.

Trigger	Positive or Negative	What can you do?	Result
Got into an argument	*Negative*	*Talks about it*	*Fee; Better*

Trigger	Positive or Negative	What can you do?	Result

Trigger	Positive or Negative	What can you do?	Result

Chapter 7

Consider life as being one frame at time

Think of your life being like an old movie
when it is one frame at a time. Each frame is
about one second. Take an example; you got
into an argument with your girlfriend. Well
there was at one time before the argument you
two was getting along just fine. Now lets us
take a look at your situation taking one frame at
a time.

<table>
<tr><td>Every thing
is just fine

1st frame</td><td>You and
your
girlfriend
start to talk
2nd frame</td><td>You was
suppose to
meet here
earlier

3rd frame</td></tr>
</table>

She got mad
at you
because you
forgot

4th frame

The two of
you get into
an argument

5th frame

The two of
you broke
up

6th frame

Let us take a good look at these 6 frames and let's determine who may be at wrong.

First Frame everything is fine

Second Frame the two of them started to talk

Third Frame Told her boyfriend that he was supposed to meet her earlier

Fourth Frame The girl friend got mad because the guy just forgot to meet her

Fifth frame both of them are into an argument

Six Frame the two of them broke up

In my opinion by looking at the third and fourth frame it was the guys fault because he admitted that he forgot he was supposed to meet her before. We don't know what is in-between the fourth and fifth frame to determine who was at fault for them to break up. It is important that we take time out when we get mad at one another or have any kind of problems. This is a good way to take one frame at a time to determine what could have been done differently.

Chapter 8

Exercise

You do not have to go to a gym to exercise.
All you have to do it take a walk. If it is bad
weather, then go to a mall near you. Walking is
the best exercise you can do. Before you do any
exercise be sure to check with your doctor.

Below write down what exercise you can do:

Exercise	Times per Week	Minutes

Chapter 9

It's time to Relax

It is good to take some time out to relax.

Find some time into what you like to. Such as

the following:

Listen to Music	Meditation	Yoga
Take a long walk	Deep breathing	Pets
gardening	Cooking	Spending some quiet time
Pray	Read the Bible	Religious study
Reading	Watching Tv	Volunteering
Go to the Movies	Talk with a friend	Writing
Drawing	Painting	Play an instrument
Go for a ride in the car	Singing	Watch a funny movie

On the next page fill in the blanks as to what
you like to do.

Activity	Times per Week	Minutes

Chapter 10

Seeing your Therapist

Seeing a therapist on a regular basis is a good idea because it can help you to talk about your problems of everyday life. Your therapist can help you cope with your feelings, problem solve and change your behaviors which could be contributing to your symptoms. You would want to track your moods, keep a journal. This way you can bring it when you see your therapist. You can bring this book with you so you can go over what you wrote in it.

Seeing a therapist can help you in the following ways:

- Cope with any stressors in your life

- Help you reach your wellness goals

- Understand better your mental health condition

- Help you overcome your fears

- Help you to work thru past traumatic experiences

- Identify triggers

- Help you to improve your relationships with family or friends

- Help you to develop a plan for coping when you are in a crisis

- Talk about your symptoms

- Discus any thought of hurting yourself or someone else

Remember when you see your therapist it is confidential except if one is either suicidal or homicidal.

When you first start to see your therapist, you may want to see him/her on more of a regular basis. This may be once a week or every other week depending on their schedule.

Fill in what your short term and long-term goals are.

Short Term Goals	Long term Goals

Chapter 11

Wellness Strategies

Wellness strategies are things that you can do to keep you well and maintain your daily living. They can include going for walks, journaling, seeing a friend. Below write down some wellness strategies that you can do:

Wellness Strategy

Chapter 12

How to handle setbacks

We all may have some setbacks from time to time. Take a look back in this book on how you handle setbacks. I know I am getting depressed when I self-isolate, stay indoors and avoid people. That happened to me recently, so I know what helped me before. I started to go back to our self-help center. This way I got out and be amongst people.

Write down on the next page what setbacks you have and what can you do when this happens:

Set Back	What can you do?

Whenever you feel you are experiencing a setback it is a good idea to look back at other times you have experienced a setback. The key thing is to keep busy. Keep your mind active. You can do this by getting out of your apartment or house. Make sure you get out of bed at the same time each day and try to go to sleep at the same time. Get some exercise each day even if it just means to talk a walk. Walking is a good way to help balance the chemicals in the brain. Once you get in the habit of walking it will just become a routine. If you can do other exercises by all means take advantage and work out an exercise schedule.

Chapter 13

Journaling

A good way to help you vent your feelings is by journaling. Take time out each day and write about something you did during the day. By writing down your thoughts you will be able to make more sense out of your day. You will be able to keep track of your highs and your lows. Perhaps you may even find a mistake that you did during the day where if you did not write about it you would have never realized it.

Why do people journal? You may not realize it but by writing down your thoughts you may be able to solve a problem or remember something

you have done differently the day before. This

will come in handy for a reference on how to

maintain the different problems you have. It is

also a good way to problem solve. So why not

make journaling a part of your day each day.

Do not worry although if you did not have time

to write in you journal on one day. Just pick up

where you left of the next day.

Below are some examples you may want to put in your journal:

- What makes you happy
- What happened today that made you feel good
- What was the worst thing that happened today to you
- What do I like about myself?
- What do I not like about myself?
- What are the stressors in my life?
- What helps me with stressors in my life?
- What was the low part of my day today?
- What was the high part of my day today?

- What was the best thing that happened in
  my life?

- What was the worst thing that happened in
  my life?

- Make a personal inventory of yourself
  (Good and Bad)

- What can you do to help yourself on a
  daily basis?

- Where would you like to live?

Chapter 14

Create a support network for yourself

It is very important that you create a support network of your friends, family or co-workers. These are people who see you pretty much on a daily basis. Sometimes we cannot see ourselves and how we react to problems each day. We may seem to be feeling good however perhaps our friends can see us in a different way. We cannot really tell if we are in a manic stage. We may seem to be perfectly fine but to others they see how we act.

Have caring people you can count on in time
of need. It is a good idea to develop your
support network when you are feeling good.
Talk to them and tell them what your wishes are
should you be back sliding in your illness. Tell
them about this book you have written and even
go over it with them. Trust me if they really
care about you they will take the time out to help
you.

Develop a good support plan as we discussed
in earlier chapters of this book. Go over the plan
with your support network.

Another good place to find people for your
support network are at support groups. There

are usually a Self-Help Center in every county

within the United States. This is another good

place to in list some people for your support

network. This is a good place because they have

firsthand experience with mental illness. You

will find all types of people with all types of

illnesses. Do not be shy, open up when you are

ready to in your meetings. The more you share

with people that you can trust the better you will

feel. Like I explained in earlier chapters how we

become a pressure cooker. When we hold things

in and do not release our feelings it is time to

blow our stack. Trust me from my own

experience I feel much better when I share and

open up in my support meetings. Also, I listen

to other people and they may just be going thru

the same thing I am.

Chapter 15

Educate yourself

The best way you can help yourself is by

learning about your illness. Many Self-Help

Centers have courses or groups on different

subjects of mental health. If you are up to it,

you can even take a course at your county

college in your area. I never thought about

going back to school. On September of 2005 I

went to college for my first time. At the time I

was 50 years old, so you can never be too old to

go back to school. I really enjoyed learning and

I did better in college than I did in High School.

I applied myself more and with the life learning

experience I had paid off. At the present time I am ¾ way for my Associates Degree in Psych and Rehab.

With the education I have and life experience I can tell when I am starting to feel depressed or start to back slide in my illness. The good thing about that is once I realize it I know what I need to do to get myself back on track.

Chapter 16

Develop a Healthy Lifestyle

To stay well sometimes may mean to change your lifestyle. With mental illness we need to take our medications as prescribed on a daily basis. Get as much of light as you can. I know when the fall comes in and it gets dark earlier I suffer from SAD (Seasonal Affective Disorder). You can experience the following symptoms as daylight decreases during the winter months:

- Depression

- Hard getting out of bed in the morning

- Difficulty concentrating

- Difficulty focusing

- Difficulty getting motivated

- Drop in energy level

- Weight gain

- Sleep more than usual

- Less socializing

As soon as spring starts to come around I feel different. I have more energy, less depressed wanting to get out and do things.

A good and healthy lifestyle is maintaining both your physical and mental health. The more you are able to do the better. However, be careful do not over do it.

Below make a list of things you enjoy doing

out doors:

Below make a list you like to do indoors if it

is a rainy day and you cannot go outside:

Exercise on a daily basis. Even if it is just for a few minutes. Each day increase the time you spend. Exercising helps in many ways such as:

- Reduces insomnia

- Helps with symptoms of Depression

- Helps with Anxiety

- Improves concentration and memory

- Helps to increase self-esteem

Try to exercise 20 minutes a day. Once you develop a routine it will come naturally for you to exercise. Make a list of exercises you like to do.

Exercises I like to do

Dieting is an important part to wellness. Make a daily menu and stick to it. With the combination of exercising and dieting you will lose weight and feel much better.

Sleep is another part to your wellness routine. Try to develop a certain time each night you go to sleep. Lack of sleep worsens mania and depression. If you have a history of manic episodes and lose a night sleep, call you doctor right away. You need to get a good night sleep every night. That is why it is important to keep active during the day. If you nap too much during the day you will not be able to sleep at night. Sometimes you have to push yourself to stay awake. It can be hard if you work on different shifts each week. By the time the end of the week is you are used to that sleep schedule. Then you have to start all over again with a different time you go to sleep. If possible, try to work the same hours each week. Below are healthy habits to help you get a good night's sleep:

- Avoid caffeine

- Avoid use of nicotine three hours before bedtime

- Avoid use of alcohol

- Eat on a regular schedule

- Exercise daily, this will help you fall asleep naturally

- Avoid exercise or any strenuous activity before going to bed

- Keep a routine so your body knows when it is time to go to sleep

- Avoid taking long naps during the day time

- Consider sex for relaxation

- Use your bedroom for sleep and sex only

- Sleep in a space that is not too noisy or too much light. The darker the better.

- Avoid any stressful situations before going to sleep

I use YouTube which has sleep meditation. This helps me a lot to fall asleep. Next thing I now it and it is the next morning. I use headphones to I can get the full effect. It is very important that you get a good night's sleep. You will notice that you will start to feel better.

Chapter 17

Take time out for your self

Every once in a while, you need to take time out for yourself. Even if it is just taking a Sunday ride in the car. In the spring time you can go to parks, beaches or any other place you would like to go to. Getting outside is the best medicine one can do for themselves. I myself like to go to parks and walk on the paths. I like to go camping whenever I can. Being outside and getting the proper amount of sun is good for the you. The sun produces Vitamin D which helps balance the chemicals in the brain.

Write down some things you like to do outdoors:

Chapter 18

How to stop a Panic Attack

What is a panic attack? Panic attack is fear that something is going to happen to the person. Perhaps they may fear of having a heart attack, stroke or even dying. They are caused by intense stress. the person may be having without realizing it. A panic attack is a sudden episode of intense fear that triggers severe physical reactions when there is no real danger or apparent cause. Panic attacks can be very frightening. When panic attacks occur, you might think you're losing control, having a heart attack or even dying.

Years ago, I started to have a panic attack and it was so real I thought I was having a heart attack. I was sweating, my heart was racing, chest pains

and actually felt like I was going to die. Well I went

to the emergency room thinking the worse. I started

to feel better once I got to the hospital. After the

doctor did all the necessary test I was discharged.

All of my test came back normal. I remember at the

time I was under a lot of stress. My father just

passed away and stress from my job. This was just

the start of my illness. From time to time I had the

same feelings as I did in the beginning. It was like I

was going to have a heart attack. Well I still did not

believe the doctors so I would either take myself to

the hospital or I would go by ambulance. This went

on for three years. After being admitted serval

times during the three years and all of my test

coming back normal my doctor recommended me

to see a psychiatrist. I was admitted to the behavior ward in the hospital. After attending groups during the day, I was listening to the patients and they described their symptoms. I was having the same symptoms as they were.   They were having panic attacks. So, I related to them and at that time I realized I was having panic attacks also.

Panic attacks can come on suddenly without warning. They can be very scary however they are not life threating. Once I believed I was having a panic attack and not a heart attack I was able to control it better. I was put on medication which did help. Also, I started to see a therapist. This helped me to get things off of my mind that was causing stress.

Ways to stop a panic attack:

- Hold your breath for as long as you can

- Slowly breath through the nose, exhale through the mouth

- Focus on things around you

- Think to yourself you are not going to die

- Act normal. Carry on as if you are not having a panic attack

After a while and with practice you will feel better and should have less panic attacks. Once I realized what was happening my panic attacks started to disappear.

Chapter 19

What is the difference between anxiety attack

and panic attacks?

A panic attack can come in a reaction to

stress. Having an anxiety attack a person may

feel fearful or apprehensive. They may

experience their heart racing or feel shortness of

breath. Panic attacks come on suddenly and are

extreme. Having a panic attack a person my

experience chest pains, feeling discomfort,

feeling of impending dome or actually feel like

they are going to die. On the other hand, anxiety

attacks gradually build up. The person may feel

nervous, disturbed sleep, irritability and muscle

tension. The following symptoms a person may experience during a panic attack:

- Heart palpitations, pounding heart, or accelerated heart rate

- Sweating

- Shaking

- Difficulty breathing or shortness of breath

- Feeling dizzy or light headed

- Numbness or tingling feeling

- Chills or hot flashes

- Pending dome

Anxiety Attack symptoms:

- Irritability

- Fatigue

- Dizziness feeling

- Restlessness

- Increase heart rate

- Muscle tension

- Disturbed sleep patterns

The symptoms of the two are similar. Panic attacks usually do not last too long however anxiety attacks can last longer. If untreated the both can be very debilitating. Most common treatments are medications, individual counseling and self-help strategies.   The quicker

a person gets help the better it is.

Chapter 20

What are the causes of a panic attack

A panic attack can be brought on by the following:

- Chronic stress

- Acute stress

- Traumatized by an event

- Habitual hyperventilation

- Strenuous physical activities

- Excessive caffeine intake

- Illness

- Claustrophobic

- An abrupt change of environment

I can remember when I first started to have

panic attacks my father died and our family

moved to Florida.   I was under a lot of stress at

my job. Not realizing it however all of this

started to take a toll on me. Eventually I had to

quit my job and go on disability. Eventually

when I was hospitalized for psychological

reasons I was diagnosed with major depression

and panic disorder. Once I received the proper

treatments I started to feel better. The key thing

was when I accepted my illness as being

psychological I started to feel better. It took

years however to get on the proper medications.

The quicker a person seeks help the better it is.

Chapter 21

What are the causes of an anxiety attack

The causes of anxiety attacks are similar to that of having a panic attack. As I have mentioned earlier a panic attack does not last long. The following can cause an anxiety attack:

- Stress at work

- Stress from school

- Stress in a personal relationship

- Financial stress

- Stress from an emotional trauma such as the death of a loved one

- Stress from a serious medical illness

- Side effect of a medication

- Use of recreational drugs

- Symptom of a medical illness such as: heart attack or heat stroke

- Lack of oxygen due to COPD or other lung disorders.

While having an anxiety attack a person may feel as though they are having a heart attack. They are often rushed to the emergency room. Treatment include counseling to help cope with daily problems and anti-anxiety medications.

Chapter 22

Final Thoughts

I have learned a lot over the years since I first came down with my illness. I take my medications as prescribed, see my doctors as need be and continue with counseling. Mental illness has come a long way since the 50's and 60'. It is more treatable however the key thing is getting diagnosed and seeking help right away. For three years I did not want to accept that I had a mental illness. Once I came to accept my illness the better I started to feel. I found a good psychiatrist and counselor. Once I was put on medications I was on the road to recovery.

There are a lot of new medications and test that

can be done today.

Credits

https://www.mayoclinic.org/diseases-conditions/panic-attacks/symptoms-causes/syc-20376021 3/7/2018 12:09pm

https://www.verywellmind.com/anxiety-attacks-versus-panic-attacks-2584396 3/7/2018 3:11pm

http://www.panicattackpedia.com/panic-attack-causes.html 3/7/18 4:14 pm

Living without depression & Manic Depression Mary Ellen Copeland, M.S. 1994